The Colours We Eat

Red Foods

Patricia Whitehouse

R Raintree

www.raintreepublishers.co.uk

Visit our website to find out more information about **Raintree** books.

To order:

 Phone 44 (0) 1865 888112

 Send a fax to 44 (0) 1865 314091

Visit the Raintree Bookshop at **www.raintreepublishers.co.uk** to browse our catalogue and order online.

First published in Great Britain by Raintree, Halley Court, Jordan Hill, Oxford OX2 8EJ, part of Harcourt Education.
Raintree is a registered trademark of Harcourt Education Ltd.

Editorial: Nick Hunter and Diyan Leake
Design: Sue Emerson (HL-US) and Joanna Sapwell (www.tipani.co.uk)
Picture Research: Amor Montes de Oca (HL-US) and Maria Joannou
Production: Jonathan Smith

Originated by Dot Gradations
Printed and bound in China by South China Printing Company

ISBN 1 844 21606 3
07 06 05 04 03
10 9 8 7 6 5 4 3 2 1

British Library Cataloguing in Publication Data
Whitehouse, Patricia
Red Foods
641.3
A full catalogue record for this book is available from the British Library.

Acknowledgements
The publishers would like to thank the following for permission to reproduce photographs: Amor Montes de Oca p. **23** (stone); Craig Mitchelldyer Photography pp. **20L, 20R, 21**; Dwight Kuhn pp. **10, 15**, back cover (strawberry); Fraser Photos (Greg Beck) pp. **1, 5, 6, 17, 22, 23** (sauce), **24**; Heinemann Library (Michael Brosilow) pp. **4, 7, 12, 16, 18, 19, 23** (jam, peel, seed); Rick Wetherbee p. **8**; Visuals Unlimited pp. **9** (Wally Eberhart), **13** (D. Cavagnaro), **14** (D. Cavagnaro), back cover (pepper, D. Cavagnaro).

Cover photograph of fruit and vegetables, reproduced with permission of Heinemann Library (Michael Brosilow).

 CAUTION: Children should be supervised by an adult when handling food and kitchen utensils.

Some words are shown in bold, **like this.** You can find them in the glossary on page 23.

Contents

Have you eaten red foods?

Colours are all around you.

How many different colours can you see in these foods?

All of these foods are red.

Which ones have you eaten?

What are some red fruits?

Some apples are red.

The red part of an apple is called the **peel**.

seeds

Pomegranates are red fruit.

They have lots of **seeds** inside them.

What are some red vegetables?

Some cabbages are red.

We can cook them or put them in **salads**.

This onion is red.

The part of the onion that we eat is under the red skin.

Have you tried these red fruits?

Strawberries are red and sweet.

They are tasty and good for you!

stone

Cherries are good for you, too.

Watch out for the **stones**
inside them!

Have you tried these red vegetables?

Kidney beans are small
and red.

Make sure you cook them first,
to make them soft.

These potatoes have red skins.

Did you know you can leave the skins on when you cook potatoes?

Have you tried these hot red foods?

Chilli peppers taste hot.

People use them in spicy dishes.

Red radishes are hot and crunchy.

They are tasty in **salads**.

Have you tried these soft red foods?

Strawberry **jam** is a soft red food.

Try eating it on bread or toast.

Tomato **sauce** is made by cooking tomatoes until they are soft.

It's yummy!

What drinks and soups are red?

Cranberry juice is made by squeezing the juice out of cranberries.

It's tasty and good for you!

Have you eaten beetroot soup?

The colour of the beetroot makes the soup red!

Recipe: Healthy Red Fruit Salad

❗ Ask an adult to help you.

First, wash some strawberries, cherries and raspberries.

Take out the cherry **stones**.

Next, mix all the fruit in a bowl.

Now eat your healthy red
fruit salad!

Yum!

Quiz

Can you name these red foods?

Look for the answers on page 24.

Glossary

jam
a sweet food made from fruit.
It is put on bread.

peel
skin that covers a fruit
or vegetable

sauce
a thick food that is eaten with
other food

seed
the part of a plant that grows
into another plant

salad
a cold dish made up of chopped
fruit or vegetables

stone
one hard seed inside a fruit

Index

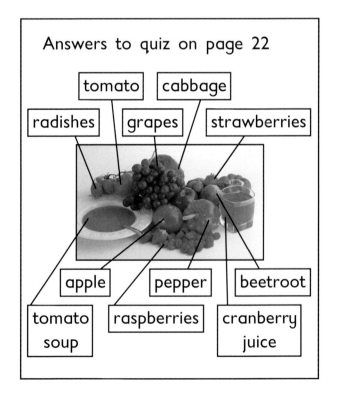

Answers to quiz on page 22

tomato   cabbage

radishes   grapes   strawberries

apple   pepper   beetroot

tomato soup   raspberries   cranberry juice

Titles in the Colours We Eat series include:

Hardback   1 844 21605 5

Hardback   1 844 21606 3

Hardback   1 844 21607 1

Hardback   1 844 21608 X

Hardback   1 844 21609 8

Hardback   1 844 21610 1

Find out about the other titles in this series on our website www.raintreepublishers.co.uk